This book belongs to

This is the story of the loaves and the fish.

You can read it alone or with anyone you wish!

There's something else. Can you guess what?

On every page there's a sparrow to spot.

The Loaves and Fish

Nick and Claire Page

Illustrations by Cathy Shimmen

make
believe
ideas

Once upon a lakeside, a long time ago,
a little boy called Benjamin
went and said "hello"
to a group of guys whose fame had spread:
Jesus and Co.

Simon and Andrew, James and John,
Philip, Bartholomew, Matthew, Tom,
another James and Simon,
and Judas 1 and 2.
This was Jesus' company – a very mixed crew!

Ben joins the crowd at sunrise.
They've come from far and wide,
hiking from the villages
into the countryside,
up into the wilderness
with Jesus as their guide.

So they keep on walking,
steady now, and slow.
Some have wished for learning
and listen as they go.
And some have wished for healing
from Jesus and Co.

Many get their wishes,
but now the sun is hot.
The crowd is feeling quite fed up –
or rather they are not.
For food is just the very thing
these people have not got.

These people have no food
and now the sun is going down.
These people need to eat
but they are nowhere near a town.
They're walking through a wilderness –
with no food to be found.

Not a bite to eat
and there are thousands to be fed.
Jesus' company tells him,
"Send them somewhere else instead.
There's nothing here: no meat, no bread.
This place is simply dead!"

"I don't know what you're talking about,"
he says. "They don't have to go.
There's plenty here for everyone,
I tell you. Don't you know?"
Easy-peasy lemon-squeezy
for Jesus and Co.!

"Oh, sure," reply his frowning friends.
"Can we buy food out here?
How are we going to pay for it?
What's the big idea?
To feed them all would cost us more
than we earn in a year!"

"Just find me a nice appetizer,"
Jesus immediately commands.
His friends go to investigate,
and see where Benny stands.
He's holding a small picnic pack,
tight between his hands.

"Could I have a word?"
says a big man named Andrew.
"Someone here called Jesus
would like to chat with you.
Come along with me now,
And bring your picnic, too."

15

So Benny goes to Jesus,
and his face is turning red.
"All I've got for supper is
five loaves of barley bread
and two small fish. It's not enough
to keep this crowd all fed."

"Don't worry, lad," says Jesus,
and he takes it from Ben's hand.
But what on earth he's up to,
Benny cannot understand.
"To feed this crowd, my picnic
really will have to expand!"

Jesus tells his friends
it's time to settle people down.
They sit in groups of fifty
on the hard but grassy ground,
hoping against hope that
somewhere food will soon be found.

Jesus lifts the barley loaves
into the evening air.
Before he dishes out the fish,
he whispers a short prayer,
thanking God, his Father,
for the food they're going to share.

At once the supper multiplies,
as Jesus says the grace!
And now there is a race
for everyone to stuff their face.
Jesus and Co. – the first to serve
fast food in this vast place!

Benjamin's astounded!
Says aloud, "How can it be
that Jesus made my picnic
feed this king-size family?"
He's made a meal of miracles!
It's a mystery to me!"

21

"Has everybody had enough?
Don't stand there twiddling your thumbs.
There's seconds here for everyone!"
cries Jesus to his chums.
They pick up all the leftovers
in twelve big baskets. Crumbs!

That night, Benjamin goes home
and gets into his bed.
Tells his mom about his day:
five thousand people fed.
"Jesus and his company
are the best thing since sliced bread!"

High up on the mountainside,
a long time ago,
Benny saw a miracle —
a wonderful show.
But that was quite the normal thing
for Jesus and Co.

Simon and Andrew, James and John,
Philip, Bartholomew, Matthew, Tom,
another James and Simon,
and Judas 1 and 2.
This was Jesus' company —
one you can join, too!

Ready to tell

Oh no! Some of the pictures from this story have been mixed up! Can you retell the story and point to each picture in the correct order?

Picture dictionary

Encourage your child to read these harder words from the story and gradually develop their basic vocabulary.

basket   bread   crowd

fish   friends   grass

groups   village   wilderness

Key words

Here are some key words used in context. Help your child to use other words from the border in simple sentences.

People **are** listening to Jesus.

Jesus taught **in** many places.

Jesus prays **to** God.

"You **can** have my picnic," says Ben.

There is enough food **for** everyone.

Make some yummy savory bread

This easy-to-make dish of fish and bread may not feed five thousand, but it makes a yummy snack for a party.

You will need

2 cloves garlic, peeled and crushed • ½ lb peeled shrimp • chives, freshly chopped • ¼ lb butter • 1 long French loaf • a large bowl • a bread knife • a teaspoon

What to do

1 Preheat the oven to 400°F.

2 Put the butter in the bowl. Make sure it is soft.

3 Add the shrimp, garlic, butter, and chives. Stir everything together until the ingredients are well mixed.

4 With a grown-up's help, make cuts in the bread about ½ in apart. It's important not to cut all the way through.

5 Spoon the shrimp and herb butter evenly into each cut.

6 Wrap the bread in foil and ask a grown-up to help you put it in the oven (and take it out again). Bake for 5–10 minutes.

7 Remove from the oven, carefully remove the foil and put on a serving dish or tray. Beware, it will be hot. Serve and enjoy!